GUINEA PIGS
ARE NOT PIGS!

By Evelyn Ryan

Gareth Stevens
PUBLISHING

Please visit our website, www.garethstevens.com. For a free color catalog of all our high-quality books, call toll free 1-800-542-2595 or fax 1-877-542-2596.

Library of Congress Cataloging-in-Publication Data

Ryan, Evelyn.
Guinea pigs are not pigs!/ by Evelyn Ryan.
    p. cm. — (Confusing creature names)
Includes index.
ISBN 978-1-4824-0947-5 (pbk.)
ISBN 978-1-4824-0948-2 (6-pack)
ISBN 978-1-4824-0946-8 (library binding)
1. Guinea pigs Juvenile literature. I. Title.
SF459.G9 R93 2015
636.935—d23

Published in 2015 by
Gareth Stevens Publishing
111 East 14th Street, Suite 349
New York, NY 10003

Copyright © 2015 Gareth Stevens Publishing

Designer: Michael J. Flynn
Editor: Greg Roza

Photo credits: Cover Miroslav Hlavko/Shutterstock.com; p. 5 (guinea pig) Kosobu/Shutterstock.com; p. 5 (pig) Bildagentur Zoonar GmbH/Shutterstock.com; p. 7 (beaver) Brian Lasenby/Shutterstock.com; p. 7 (guinea pig teeth) Photo Fun/Shutterstock.com; p. 7 (mouse) Ziga Camernik/Shutterstock.com; p. 9 djem/Shutterstock.com; p. 11 UniversalImagesGroup/Getty Images; p. 13 wiwsphotos/Shutterstock.com; p. 15 Christian Prandl/Getty Images; p. 17 kerstiny/Shutterstock.com; p. 19 Thomas Schneider/Getty Images; p. 21 Marina Jay/Shutterstock.com.

Printed in the United States of America

CPSIA compliance information: Batch #CS15GS: For further information contact Gareth Stevens, New York, New York at 1-800-542-2595.

CONTENTS

Boldface words appear in the glossary.

What Is It?

Guinea pigs are cute little animals that many people keep as pets. In some places, people eat them! This furry critter isn't actually a pig. If guinea pigs aren't pigs, then what are they? Read on to find out!

pig

guinea pig

5

Guinea Pigs Are Rodents!

A rodent is a small, furry animal with long front teeth. These teeth never stop growing. Guinea pigs and other rodents keep their teeth sharp by gnawing on wood and other plants. Rodents make up about half of all the **mammals** in the world.

guinea pig teeth

mouse

beaver

Where Are They?

Originally, guinea pigs were wild animals from South America. There are no wild guinea pigs anymore, but they're closely **related** to several kinds of wild rodents. Today, guinea pig pets can be found in people's homes all over the world.

9

On the Farm

People first started living with guinea pigs around 5,000 years ago! At that time, people in South America began using the rodents for food. They put guinea pigs in pens so they wouldn't run away, just like we do today with chickens.

Eating Veggies

Guinea pigs spend a lot of their time gnawing and eating. They eat most kinds of vegetables, but they love leafy green vegetables. They get most of the water they need from the plants they eat.

Noisy Pigs!

Guinea pigs may have gotten their name from the noises they make. They **squeal** like pigs do, sometimes very loudly! They often do this when they think they're about to be fed. Depending on how they feel, guinea pigs also click their teeth, **growl**, and purr.

15

Guinea Pig Families

Female guinea pigs can have babies several times a year. They usually have about four babies at a time, but they can have up to 14! Guinea pigs grow quickly. They usually live 3 to 5 years, but some live up to 8 years.

I'm No Guinea Pig!

Have you ever heard someone say they were treated like a guinea pig? That means they were used to test something new. Guinea pigs have long been used to study and test new **products**. This has helped keep people safe, but many people think it's **cruel**.

Piggy Pets

Guinea pigs are popular pets. They're easy to care for. They're also very friendly. Once they're used to you, you can pick them up and pet them. Guinea pigs don't usually bite people. It might happen if they mistake your finger for a carrot!

Caring for Guinea Pigs

Guinea pigs like room to run around. Make sure their cage isn't too small.

Spread wood chips on the bottom of the cage. Guinea pigs like to hide in them. Change the wood chips about every week (or they will get stinky!).

Guinea pigs like company, so you can keep more than one in a cage. However, males may fight.

Feed your guinea pigs food from a pet store. They can also eat vegetables. Make sure they always have water.

Guinea pigs love to munch on grass all the time. This helps keep their teeth short.

Guinea pigs love to play! Give them small boxes and paper towel tubes to crawl through and hide in.

GLOSSARY

cruel: mean and causing pain

growl: a low sound many animals make

mammal: a warm-blooded animal that has a backbone and hair, breathes air, and feeds milk to its young

product: something made or grown that is offered for sale

related: animal groups that share common features

squeal: a high sound many animals make

FOR MORE INFORMATION

BOOKS

Beck, Angela. *Guinea Pigs: Keeping and Caring for Your Pet.* Berkeley Heights, NJ: Enslow Publishers, 2013.

Carraway, Rose. *Great Guinea Pigs.* New York, NY: Gareth Stevens, 2012.

Petrylak, Ashley. *Guinea Pigs.* New York, NY: Marshall Cavendish Benchmark, 2010.

WEBSITES

Guinea Pig Care
www.aspca.org/pet-care/small-pet-care/guinea-pig-care
Learn how to care for guinea pigs and decide if they are a good pet for you.

Rodents
animal.discovery.com/mammals/rodents.htm
Learn about the many different kinds of rodents in the world, including the cavies.

INDEX